Superstart cello

accompaniments
piano accompaniments and cello duet parts

**Mary Cohen
and Robert Spearing**

For use with **Superstart Cello**

FABER ***ff*** MUSIC

Teacher's note

In this book you will find a mixture of piano accompaniments and cello duet parts. Some of the pieces in the pupil's book need no accompaniment and it is hoped that the resulting combination of accompanied and unaccompanied pieces will be useful for performance in a variety of settings. The page reference for the pupil's book is given in brackets at the end of each line in the contents list.

© 2006 by Faber Music Ltd
This edition first published in 2006
3 Queen Square London WC1N 3AU
Music processed by Jeanne Roberts
Cover and text design by Susan Clarke
Printed in England by Caligraving Ltd

ISBN 0-571-52443-5

Contents

Asturias

Encourage the pupil to copy the dynamics in the piano accompaniment
The left hand may be played on its own as a cello accompaniment (pizz.)

Isaac Albéniz
arr. Mary Cohen

Habañera

Encourage the pupil to copy the dynamics in the piano accompaniment

Georges Bizet
arr. Mary Cohen

Norwegian dance

Encourage the pupil to copy the dynamics in the piano accompaniment

Edvard Grieg
arr. Mary Cohen

March of the kings

Encourage the pupil to copy the dynamics in the piano accompaniment

Georges Bizet
arr. Mary Cohen

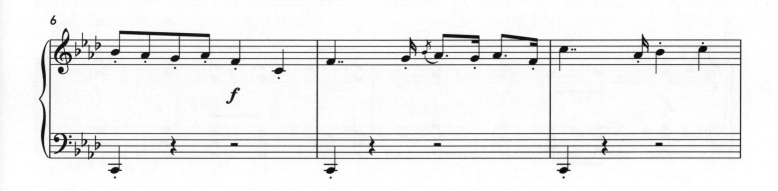

*Swing arm away from the string each time

Banana bubble gum

Thoinot Arbeau
arr. Robert Spearing, adapted Mary Cohen

Allegretto ♩ = 66

Beasties

Active ants! Active ants!

Mary Cohen

Dozing dino snores *Encourage the pupil to copy the dynamics in the piano part*

Mary Cohen

Galloping gazelles *Encourage the pupil to copy the dynamics in the piano part*

Mary Cohen

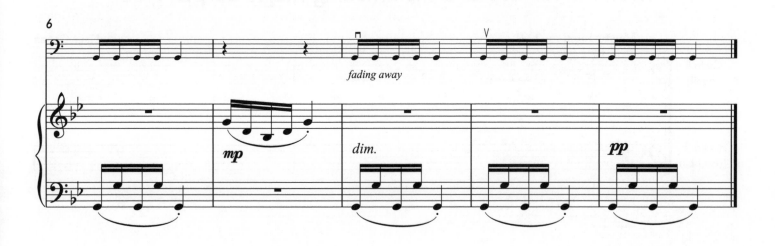

Crocodile crawl *Encourage the pupil to copy the dynamics in the piano part*

Mary Cohen

Mister Misterioso and his amazing magic carpet ride

Mary Cohen

Last time get quieter and quieter,
as the carpet flies out of sight

The good sound guide

Mary Cohen

Enthusiastically ♩ = 100

Cello 1 (pupil)

Cello 2 (teacher)

Play:

Horrid D string sounds

1. If you grip you'll make a scri – tchy scra – tchy sound.
2. Too much ro – sin makes an it – ty grit – ty sound.
3. If you skid you'll make an ea – ky squea – ky sound.

Horrid D string sounds

If you grip you'll make a scri – tchy scra – tchy sound.
Too much ro – sin makes an it – ty grit – ty sound.
If you skid you'll make an ea – ky squea – ky sound.

Horrid D string sounds

If you grip you'll make a scri – tchy scra – tchy sound.
Too much ro – sin makes an it – ty grit – ty sound.
If you skid you'll make an ea – ky squea – ky sound.

Play with a really good sound!

Chorus

Let your fin – gers float. Flex your fin – gers and your
Just go down, up, down.
Keep your bow – ing straight.

thumb, please. Flex your fin – gers and your thumb, please.

Flex your fin – gers and your thumb, please, and the sound will just come out.

The song of the Australian bee eater

Mary Cohen & Robert Spearing

*Pupil can pause here to read out thought bubbles.

A day in the life of an octopus

The octopus wakes up . . .

The octopus yawns and stretches . . .

The octopus goes downstairs . . .

Treading carefully ♩ = 66

The octopus munches breakfast . . .

Munching steadily ♩ = 66

The octopus has a busy time at work . . .

Watching carefully ♩ = 69

mf

The octopus comes back home . . .

Trying to stop eyelids drooping ♩ = 60

mp *legatissimo*

con Ped.

Maybe Abey Astronaut

Mary Cohen & Robert Spearing

Misterioso ♩ = 52

Play as smoothly as possible

Maybe Ab - ey As - tro - naut is up in space... May - be through a te - le - scope I'd

con Ped.

see his face! May - be Ab - ey As - tro - naut is look - ing down...

poco sf

poco sf

poco rit.

May - be Ab - ey As - tro - naut can see my town!

glissando lightly, very, very quietly up and down the fingerboard

Strange friends (lurking in the witch's house)

Batty bats

Mary Cohen

Weird ♩ = 72

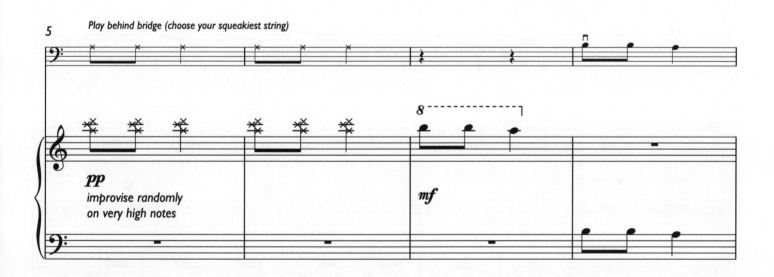

Play behind bridge (choose your squeakiest string)

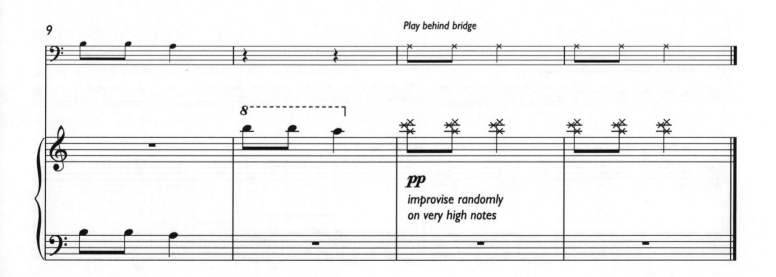

Play behind bridge

20

Ratty rats

Menacing ♩ = 66

. . . And black, black cats

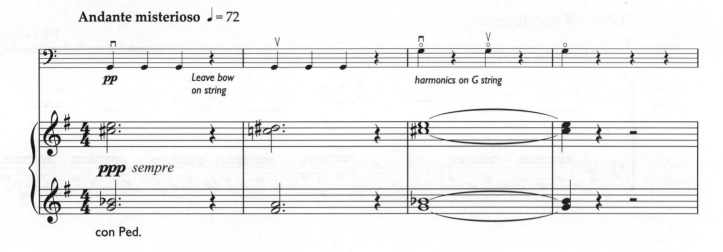

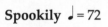

Not forgetting . . . spindly, spooky spiders

Gruesome grub

Stir-fried centipedes

Mary Cohen
(adapted from Robert Spearing)

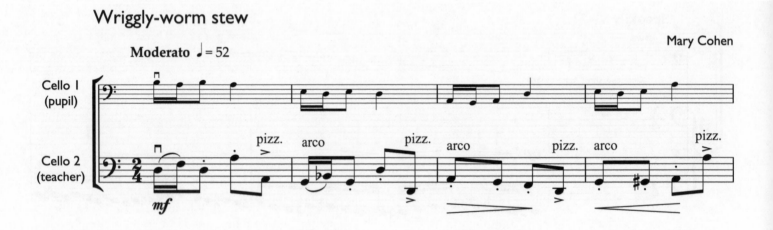

Wriggly-worm stew

Mary Cohen

Caterpillar dumplings

Mary Cohen

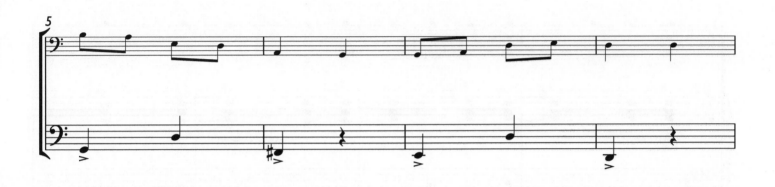

Captain Fortissimo and his fire engine

Mary Cohen & Robert Spearing

Awkward moments

Feeling awkward

Mary Cohen

Oops...

Mary Cohen

On the warpath ♩ = 72

Old MacDonald had the blues

Mary Cohen & Robert Spearing

Twinkle, twinkle, little bat

Mary Cohen & Robert Spearing

Gloomy ♩ = 60 *(like a tea tray with spilt tea sloshing all over it...)*

con Ped.

Brightening up again *(optional: get gradually faster and faster)*

Monsieur Arbeau's sword dance

Thoinot Arbeau
arr. Robert Spearing

Brother Jack eats hot croissants by the light of the moon

Moderato (*setting off with the croissants*) ♩ = 46

Mary Cohen & Robert Spearing

Andante (*gazing at the moon*) ♩ = 54

Rocky mountain

Traditional
arr. Mary Cohen

Merrily we roller blade

Traditional
arr. Mary Cohen & Robert Spearing

Flowing ♩ = 63

mp Mer – ri – ly we rol – ler blade, rol – ler blade, rol – ler blade.

3

Mer – ri – ly we rol – ler blade, try – ing not to knock too ma – ny peo – ple o – ver.

1. *Ending for verse 1*

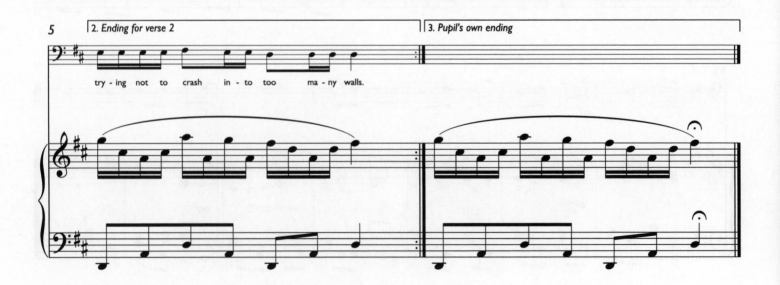

5

2. *Ending for verse 2*

try – ing not to crash in – to too ma – ny walls.

3. *Pupil's own ending*

Ho la hi

Traditional
arr. Mary Cohen & Robert Spearing

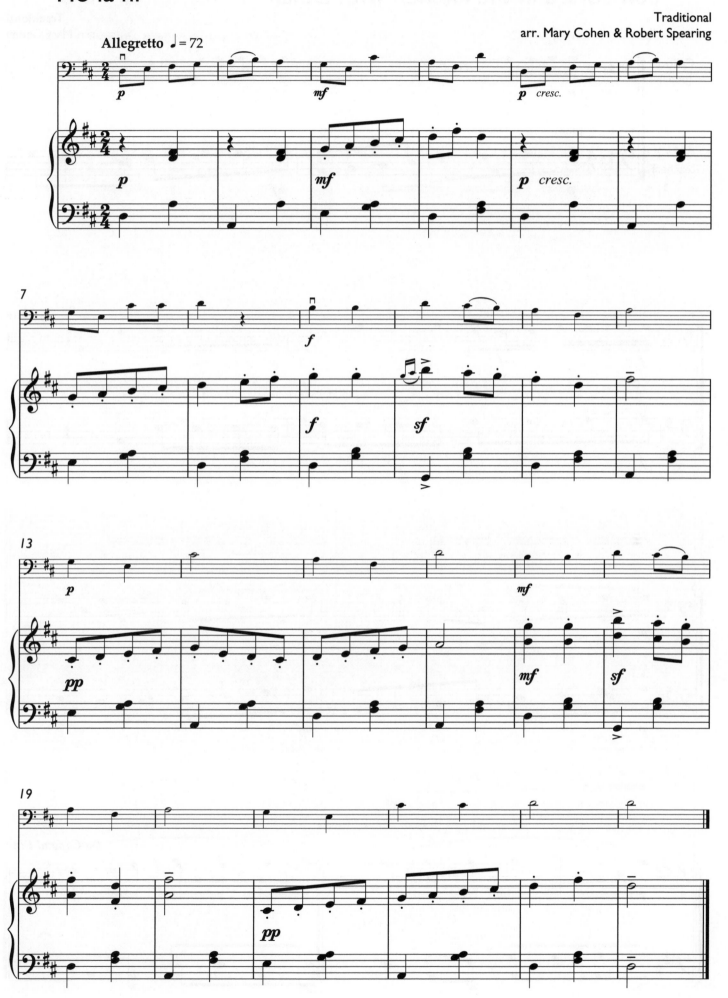

Someone's in the kitchen with Dinah

Traditional
arr. Mary Cohen

Turkey in the straw

Traditional
arr. Mary Cohen & Robert Spearing

Riddle song from Hansel and Gretel

Engelbert Humperdinck
arr. Robert Spearing

1. A lit - tle man is stand - ing with - in the wood. He
2. The lit - tle man is si - lent and makes no sound. He

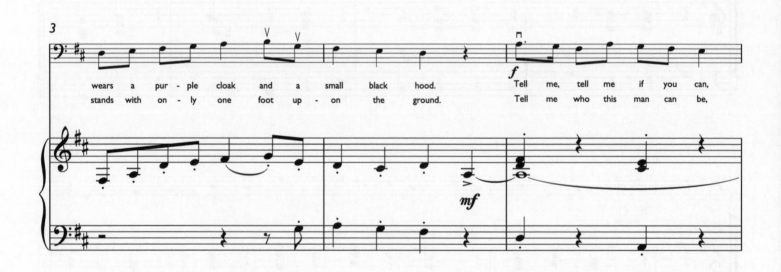

wears a pur - ple cloak and a small black hood. Tell me, tell me if you can,
stands with on - ly one foot up - on the ground. Tell me who this man can be,

What's the name of this small man? In a pur - ple cloak and a small black hood.
For he will not an - swer me, Stand - ing there with one foot up - on the ground.

Alouette

Traditional
arr. Mary Cohen

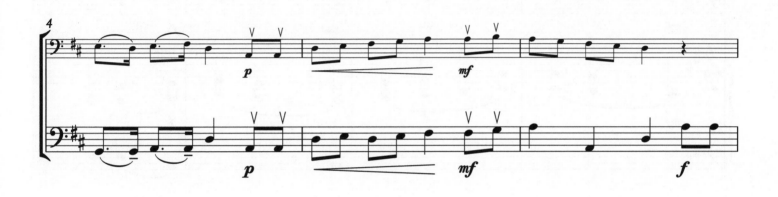

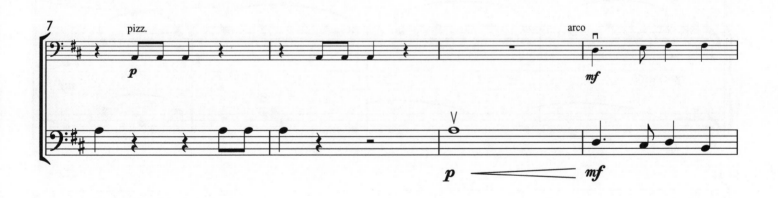

Theme from the Choral Symphony

Ludwig van Beethoven
arr. Robert Spearing

Largo from the New World Symphony

Antonin Dvořák
arr. Robert Spearing

All mixed up!

Moderato ♩ = 120

Mary Cohen & Robert Spearing

Oh __ some - times I feel hap - py and __ some - times I feel sad. Oh __

some - times I be - have so well and __ some - times I'm plain bad. I'm __

all mixed up (I'm a mixed - up pup) but I want to be quite or - di - na - ry... So to-

- day I'll just feel hap - py, and __ then we'll all be glad! (Hooray!)

Swing low, sweet chariot (C major version)

Traditional
arr. Mary Cohen

Jumbo, a-limberin' up of a mornin'

Mary Cohen

Falling asleep in the rocking chair

Mary Cohen

Kalinka

Traditional
arr. Robert Spearing

Migildi, magildi

Traditional
arr. Mary Cohen

Rondeau

Henry Purcell
arr. Robert Spearing